Also by the author

Poetry
Grub
Rasputin and His Children
Blue Lamp Disco

As editor
Map-Makers' Colors:
New Poets of Northern Ireland
(co-edited with Todd Swift)

THE RESURRECTION OF THE BODY AT KILLYSUGGEN

THE RESURRECTION OF THE BODY AT KILLYSUGGEN

MARTIN MOONEY

30/3/12.

LAGAN PRESS
BELFAST
2011

Acknowledgements
Some of these poems have appeared in *The Black Mountain Review*, *The Frogmore Papers*, *Iota*, *Magma*, *Poetry Ireland Review*, *The Red Wheelbarrow*, *The Slab*, and *The Yellow Nib*.

'Postcards from Zakynthos' was written for and first appeared in *From the Small Back Room: A Festschrift for Ciaran Carson* (Netherlea Press, 2009)

'History, *or*, the Wrestling Bills' was one of a group of poems drawn from the archives of Belfast's Ulster Hall commissioned for the Hall's re-opening in 2009.

Most of the phrases quoted in '6,781 Rules for the Elimination of Accidents' are taken from *Towards the Elimination of Human Error* by Bob Gourley (no publisher given, 2002).

'*In Memoriam* Les Gray' quotes from 'Oh Boy', written by Norman Petty, Bill Tilghman and Sunn West.

A grant from Newtownabbey Borough Council made possible a stay at the Tyrone Guthrie Centre in Annaghmakerrig, Co Monaghan, where this collection began to come together. Thanks to both organisations.

And many thanks to Peter Haining for introducing me to the work of Moscow Joe McKinley.

Published by
Lagan Press
Unit 45
Westlink Enterprise Centre
30-50 Distillery Street
Belfast BT12 5BJ
e-mail: lagan-press@e-books.org.uk
web: lagan-press.org.uk

ARTS COUNCIL of Northern Ireland

ISBN: 978 1 908188 00 7 (pbk)
978 1 904652 01 4 (hbk)
Author: Mooney, Martin
Title: The Resurection of the Body at Killysuggen
2011

Us? What do we look like?
Send us back the pictures so that we can see.

—Mairtín Crawford

CONTENTS

THE HUMOURS OF BALLYCRAN

'It would bring tears to the eyes of a turnip,' said a man in
his cups
holding on for dear life to the bar in The Saltwater Brig,
'to see the state of the roads at Six Road Ends, and the grass
that grows
through the cracks in the runways of Kirkiston airbase—

though it's many's the long day since the last American rose
into the low skies above a derelict cottage in Ballycranbeg,
and left the field to the racing drivers and long-footed
Irish hare,
the one a bestial roar, the other a whisper in long grass.

Now I'm told I've as much chance of kissing again—
at my age, in my condition—as there is of that crab-apple tree
sprouting nine-pound notes, or nuns coming back to
Nuns Quarter,
or a puma or panther stalking the hills of the County Down.

And if that came to pass, wouldn't they scour the Low Country
with their marksmen and nets, their guns and their helicopters,
and wouldn't the poor thing be hunted down and put to death?
So I'll act my age,' he said, 'and I'll keep my lips to myself.'

THE BALLAD OF MOSCOW JOE

In the war of words between Philomena
Begley and Susan McCann—who was who and which
 was queen
of Irish country music—I lost two figurine-

encrusted art-cars, torched by yobs with a grudge
against what's beautiful. That was the thick end of a wedge
that had seen my wife abandon our marriage

as well as the bungalow I glorified with collaged nick-
nacks, doctored garden ornaments, *objets trouvés*, hand-picked
junk, notices to the world in general and Carnlough

in particular. To her it was nothing but *Merz*,
to me it was—as she had been—a way of living with the world's
embarrassment of riches without it breaking our hearts.

Which are born broken: all this stuff, these assemblages
and amateur road-signs, is just the wages
of heartbreak, and when my children launch their purge

it will be swept away: as Philomena might well sing,
this ain't my home unless you wear my ring.
So bulldoze the bungalow. All this furious decorating

was only ever meant to reconcile me to the lack
of ... Well, when country music's played in reverse on a
 tape deck,
your truck starts, your dog gets better, your girl comes back.

HISTORY, *or*, THE WRESTLING BILLS

the wrestling bills
on a Friday night
top stars
like Tommy Mann

ack them were the days
the old Troubles
killed all that and
the punk rockers

they disgust me
you should see them
pulling off their shirts
and spitting

BELFAST FROM SPACE

You might, as the man said, imagine a lobster
with its tail flexed along the Lagan
and a pincer stretched on both shores of the Lough,

or again, picture a shower of Neolithic
lads and lasses stranded on a sandbar, bickering
about whose fault, whose stupid fault, it is

that they are so far out on a withered limb
they might as well be on the moon
or whatever they call that moon-face in the sky.

In this satellite photo of Belfast from space
I can see the street you lived on, and my own street.
It's the ultimate out-of-body experience,

up there with acid or *amanita*, or *Romper*
Room's Miss Helen reading out the names
of all the kids she claimed to see

through the spiral galaxy of her magic mirror—
psychedelia on black and white TV—
though her Martin was always a different Martin.

Nostalgia. Google Earth. Shamanic journeys.
I can't come with you, but I wish you luck.
I'm a pop artist, not a visionary.

The older I get, the more I stay at home.
Or as Moscow Joe McKinley would have had it,
I'm crap to know. I'm an oul show-off

in summer, but in long dark winter
a pathetic geek ... The night's a wreath
of orbital debris and exoplanets.

Armagh's stargazers saw through cloud
to the transit of Venus, a beauty spot
on the thermonuclear breast

of the sun. By such a tiny blemish
whole worlds, like ours perhaps, are known.
Plugged into life support, the deep coma

of suspended animation, who knows
how long you'd take to get there?
As far as you're concerned, no time at all.

As Christ said, in one of the worst
jokes about the crucifixion, I
can see your house from here. Driving

the M1's lobster-tail to meet my girl,
the City Cemetery where you're buried
is at my shoulder like a navigator.

How often did we steer home
by the stars, half-cut, on autopilot?
Once too often, or one time too few?

RADIO ULSTER NEWS

I was leaving no stone unturned in my granny's bedroom,
in search of the savings the old cow had salted away

against the expense of her Co-op pauper's funeral,
when the radio said that the body dragged from the dam

and decayed almost beyond identification
was that of my brother, unheard-from these past three years,

since his card had been marked and he'd had his
    marching orders
from my father-in-law, his wife and the rest of the boys.

CONNOLLY WINDOW

With your nose pressed against a stained glass window
portraying James Connolly tied to a kitchen chair
with a target pinned to his heart like a Poppy Day poppy,

you're either an honoured guest in the Lord Mayor's parlour
watching smoke clear from the grounds of City Hall,
or peering in from outside as the shade of Winnie Carney,

fresh from a night of markswomanship and shorthand,
waltzes her ex-Orangeman husband, her red Prod,
on marble floors—and it was far from marble you were reared.

BANNING *FRANKENSTEIN*

Belfast, 1932

The Wee Yard in the ice age. The slips are concrete
glaciers plunged in the Lough. You expect

the oily water to flash-freeze, or boil and rage,
but nothing happens. Cranes like laboratory

clamps or lightning-catchers bristle overhead
but the cloud is limp. Yes we have no bananas

no money no piano in the parlour but at least
there is no poverty under the blankets.

We make love to breed more idle hands,
of course we do. There is safety in numbers.

The indoor bathtub bathes a hoard of coal
while our children go barefoot and foul-mouthed

in the cinderbowls of last year's bonfires.
They flock to hear the mad scientists of the gospel

preach the Good News: if God had ever loved us,
He would have made us wealthy men, elsewhere.

Whose hand is this? When was it branded
D for *Deib*? Why have I woken
in this town of smoke and open drains

whose citizens gather at churches and dead
manufactories enraged by something
I seem to have done in a previous life?

Die Erbsünde. I have inherited the inner
organs of beggars, traitors, insolent apprentices.
My right eye is the brown eye of a heretic,

my left an atheist green. When I break free
of the crowd and make for the estuary,
I sink waist-deep in mud under the weight

of the head on my shoulders, the burden
of other people's crimes. I drag my unhealed sutures
towards the slum liberties of Ballymacarrett

where the poor lever up pavers from the street
and pile them like dark apples, eggs
fresh from the furnace and baked black.

[He] shall not reveal any of his Master's Secrets, nor conceal his loss or prejudice when known to him, but shall in due time discover and do his utmost to prevent the same. He shall not be guilty of drinking, nor accessory to any riots or tumults on the street, nor haunt idle or debauched company. He shall not walk in processions. He shall not commit fornication, nor contract Matrimony within the said term ... but shall in all respects promote his master's interests, and behave and acquit himself as becomes a faithful and diligent apprentice and shall during the whole Term aforesaid, provide all the Tools and Implements necessary for learning and practising his said Trade.

—from the Harland and Wolff apprentices' imdenture

God's is the last word on the Police Committee
but He casts His vote by proxy. We

settle our rumps on maroon velour and feast
our eyes on the hand of dusty light,

the horror on the wall. A few minutes only
makes up our minds: we must spare the citizens

this insult to the brain, and Christ this garbled
version of the Word, this anti-resurrection.

While the unemployed riot, disdaining the work-
house, raging at the means test, we narrow

our eyes our eyes our eyes rather than pluck
them out. *Mene mene tekhel upharsin.*

We padlock the picture house, but not before
we see the monster die, the screen darken,

and take this secret back to our villas
in Belmont and Strandtown, Malone, Stranmillis.

Life is a matter of electricity and original sin.
Is body parts. Ye must be born again.

MOSCOW ROAD

In the cold light of spring it's a photograph
from *Picture Post*: factories, gasometers.
Moscow Road is cutting a swathe

through wetlands towards a horizon of cranes
and windsocks, of cargo ships. There's
been a light drift of snow and the Nissen

huts are sugared with it. Nothing moves,
until a turboprop comes in to land and scares
a single pearl-grey heron from the reed beds.

It beats past Bauhaus offices, a refugee,
a ghost from the show trials, over our heads:
ration books, industry, the war years.

DREAM OF THE FISHERMAN'S WIFE

after Hokusai

The fisherman's wife's licked out by one octopus
and French-kissed by another, a tentacle
gripped in a passionate fist. It's just a dream,
she says, and not even a pleasant dream.
The fisherman is upset by the whole spectacle
and retires to his boat for a month of net-
mending, keel-scraping, caulking and sake.
It isn't just the cunnilingus

that he finds impossible to forget.
The whole human-marine genre, the tacky
fish-porn predictability of her lust
tortures his days like the refusal of the cherry
to blossom. He can't believe she loves him. But it's just
a dream, she says. I've said I'm sorry, and I'm sorry.

THE FLESH-HOOK

The witches of Islandmagee prepared
for their nights away from the marriage bed

by leaving under the eiderdown
a twist of straw or the shaft of a broom

and their husbands slept the sleep of the just;
but pity the poor man left to embrace

the Dunaverney flesh-hook: he won't know
a minute's rest for that brazen claw.

His dreams will leave him at sixes and sevens.
A family of swans? A pair of ravens?

RENDITION

The thought of you kissing your lover's chest I consign
to the frigid airspace between the vapour trails
of the plane that brings George Best's coffin to Belfast
and a CIA ghost-flight, where I will it to fade
like life leaving a body, organ by failing organ,
or the scream of a detainee thrown from the cargo hold
to fall on the parched hills of a puppet regime.

PATIENCE

For you and your lover I cook your favourite dishes—
moussaka, chicken baked in breadcrumbs—
and retire to a saint's meal of rice and asparagus,

rising at dawn to bring you breakfast in bed
and news of a brief outbreak of birdsong,
heard in the night, like a girl's cry of pleasure.

PORTRAIT OF A YOUNG NOBLEMAN HOLDING A LEMUR

for Janice

Conspirator, swordsman, amateur poet,
his pet on its silver chain has the skinniest arms
and widest eyes in the whole chateau.

Blind-looking feral glamour stares and stares
at something you can't see. Imagine
fur and weeping scullions, maps of the wars.

They don't, as a rule, live long. What will he do
when its brittle bones are buried in the keep?
Who will he find to talk to? How will he sleep?

THE RESURRECTION OF THE BODY AT KILLYSUGGEN

To think it would happen just at the dawn of winter—
querulous rooks startled from bald woods

like banknotes from a fire. We are back in our bodies
if not back in our clothes, even the dead babies

reborn in the prime of lives they'd never had,
and the old-timers struck again by sex's ambush—

the gravedigger's shed is a boudoir, but so is
every headstone, obelisk and grass-grown path.

A moss-gowned Virgin tactfully lifts her gaze
over a sandstone wall towards Bradshaw's Brae.

There are hundreds of us making love here,
all in the blink of a trumpet. In a single note from an eye.

IN THE KINGDOM OF THE BLIND

The empty vessel has a silver lining.
Clean meat is better than no bread.
Beauty never falls far from the tree.

POEM

try not to use your tongue
to investigate
the buds and folds of flesh
at its own root

NOSTALGIA

for Michael Pinnons

Have I invented, or do I remember, stumbling
on the coffin factory? How sunlight
glared on its threshold but went no further,

how boards were stacked against one wall,
and against another, coffins, lidless
and unvarnished, stood like open wardrobes.

A circular saw buzzed, and smithereens
of sawdust tumbled into the street—
and I could be wrong, but was there

a resinous bright smell of wood and glue,
and a man carrying pine in shadow
through that windowless shed, whistling?

HOKUSAI

Pushing eighty, this old man daft for art
hikes across the island to paint waves.

Finally, he thinks, mastery of his craft
is within reach—at worst, another thirty years

of looking and thinking. His eyesight's good,
his head as clear as it ever was. Still,

these waves might be his last, so he decides
to paint them male and female, tickled

to have them locked in separate panels,
all turmoil and frustration and raw difference.

You couldn't fish for tuna in those seas,
he thinks. He thinks: *too many wives, I've*

grown too cynical. And yet he can't resist
the colours brought from Europe, as he once

could not resist a pretty girl—that's gone,
he notes, that old libidinous get-up-and-go,

he's finally shed at least that much desire,
and any bitter taste is sluiced away by tides

of mauve and jewelled reds from England's
factories, of oceanic blues and greens.

He tells himself: *when I'm a hundred I shall be*
a marvellous artist, and after I am dead

a will o' the wisp taking it easy in the dark,
always in the next field, and then the next,

while more and more often, foreigners dock
their tall ships in the harbours of Japan.

THE SELF-PUBLISHED

Our mistake was writing too much
for people like ourselves, when

people like ourselves were thin
on the ground. We were all in love

with this world, that city or some wife,
but it was unrequited. Type

rattled off glass. Philosophers
say that there can't be such a thing

as a private language, and they're right.
But only by the skin of their teeth.

Put it down in your own words,
our teachers said. It was not good advice.

AVERCAMP: *SKATERS ON THE IJSSELMEER*

His lovely puritans, all dressed as witches,
glide across the river mouth in silence.
Good-living skates say *ssh* to thieves' cant,
or *tch* at dimber trulls among the saved,
morts masked as honest men. It's water off
a duck's back, double Dutch to his nibs.

To the pure all things are pure. Skiffs
lie wedged in ice like playful shipwrecks.
Icicles hang from the eaves of gospel halls.
Prepare to meet thy God. He meets his
on every expedition to the snowy world
of his studio. God of perpetual winter, God

of arm's-length white horizons, God
to think he has made a living out of this!
Do one thing, and do that one thing well.
Either the Bible or his barber-surgeon
father said that. Also, live and let live.
Hap up warm, and when your own time comes

enter the ice age of your modest art,
knowing full well that life in all its shades
of love and truth and worship will go on
without you to record it. The cold, old
friend and pew-companion that it is,
will take your fingertips. The whirr

of Calvin's arabesques will wax and wane.
Wish say the skaters, but every frost fair
ends in thaw, all church attendance
in a private journey home through streets
hushed by the snow. A last touch
of the brush, and then begin again.

APOLLINAIRE'S PORNOGRAPHY

Masturbation is an admirable thing, for it allows men and women to become accustomed to their imminent and prolonged separation.
—Guillaume Apollinaire, *Les Onze Mille Verges*

What night remains he spends on tenterhooks.
Moraine of underthings. The house itself
can't sleep for satin, jealous static, sex-smells.

Skinflint voyeur, he types up lies he thinks
might turn her on: two men and her, him with another girl.
Their lives will test the limits of invention.

Love is penurious, poetry either the old sob story,
or too much like hard work. Pornography
is a modern creature, like a Zeppelin,

or an ocean liner refitted as a hospital
where nurses flit like ghosts between the bulkheads,
unbandaging and probing open wounds.

THE ARCHITECTURE OF FIRE STATIONS

You know those hollow towers and folding
fortress doors, wide turning circles:
formal, yet common; welcoming but stern.

You know the coarse, pragmatic optimism
of the will with which the concrete's poured.
The ribbon-cutting. Will we never learn?

You know our love affairs have been like this,
built from hard-earned experience,
and each time better. Still our houses burn.

THE BARBER OF CORFU

If the barber of Corfu shaves only those
who do not shave themselves, who shaves the barber?
So many questions, it's like an inquest.
Lazarus lets his beard grow, not designer stubble
now but the real orthodox old Father William,
and his toenails too. Such perseverance.
He'd remind you of Howard Hughes, or the Steve
McQueen of the last days, down south
necking snake oil cures for cancer. Only dead.

If anyone understands what follows from
the barber paradox, it's Lazarus now: there's no
theory of everything. Only Jane Russell's bra
engineered like the Spruce Goose, the solitary
pleasure of a baseball bouncing off cement.
Six feet under, a loop of cosmic string
vibrates along his femur like a sob.
A bracelet of bright hair around the bone
it isn't. An antiphoton glancing off a razor.

THROUGH THE EYE OF A NEEDLE

What we think of as light isn't light at all,
but the shockwave sent through the stuff of the world
by one rich man passing into the Kingdom
against astronomical odds. The big bang itself
ripples out from that freak event
like the ultimate sonic boom, the deafening
gasp of a stunned God.
                                        What miracle keeps
that trauma from tearing apart the fabric
of space and time? Only the dark matter
and gravity of the world's poor. And while
they're worked to the bone, God can rest from the labour
of driving the stars into the sky's four corners.

IN MEMORIAM LES GRAY

All of my love, all of my kissin', you don't know
what you've been a-missin'. You started out
in The Mourners, and ended your days
en route to a Glasgow comeback *uh*
huh huh and throat cancer. It breaks
my 1974 heart. The fun's over, the fun's
been over for thirty years, its loss felt
more keenly with every reunion tour.
Finally, each of us is his own tribute
band, a cover version of his greatest hits.
The coffin-dodgers sing, *That's right that's right*
that's right that's right that's right that's right that's right.
Bury us all in our brothel creepers,
our hair anachronistic, our trousers tight.

PERSONAL COLUMN

In a bedsit or
studio flat above
the newsagent's
the man to blame
for the flight
of the sparrow
from our town of six
thousand souls
dissects
the last of the native
population
whose sooty breast
splits like a grape
under his razor
while on the gutter
starlings jostle for view
of the pink tongue
like a shaving
of veal he drops
into a bottle
with twenty others
and seals
with feathers
and chewed-up pages
from the personal
columns
of the local paper.

BACKWATER

for Brendan Cleary

Face south-east
through the torrent
that pours from the gutter.

Two malarial drones
at the furthest outpost
we have nothing to do

but maintain dignity,
drink gin, imagine
the odour of the local girls,

and raise each morning
a flag so worn
we can see through it.

In the end,
one of us will succumb
and trudge down the road

to the village
in search of an old *Times*
or a radio.

One of us will cough out
his last cigarette
while fog shivers

across the delta
and ask himself
if it matters.

Our joint hangovers
reunite us. The white crust
on your chapped lips

greets the vicious tremor
in my left hand.
My oldest friend,

you stiffen my resolve
with a cheery wink
and a watery gimlet.

We are in this together,
you say. We must
keep up appearances.

Our standards must not
slip any further
than they have already.

CURE

I am nipping out for a hair of the dog—
you I commend to the care of the cat,
two Nurofen, and a glass of cold water.

When I come back I will bring you fruit,
newspaper stories, cigarettes, gossip.
I am nipping out for a hair of the dog

but I won't be long, and I'll think of you
vowing you'll never touch drink again.
But two Nurofen and a glass of cold water

will be kind to your hangover—which
lets us know that more is survivable
than we imagine. My hair of the dog

will be raised in thanks that we've made it this far,
that living together is more comfort
than Nurofen and glasses of water.

Sleep well, sweetheart. I hope you don't need
these Nurofen, this glass of cold water
while I've nipped out for a hair of the dog.

6,781 RULES FOR THE ELIMINATION OF ACCIDENTS

'Think consciously at all times.'
—Bob Gourley, *Towards the Elimination of Human Error*

I continue to study the world's accident problem.
Do not drink alcoholic drinks. If you make an error when
boxing, you are quite likely to be knocked out.
Calculate when to retire to bed. Yawning is also a sign.
I have visited the homes of the great writers of the past,
and most of them worked in rooms heated by a fire.
Sometimes when walking home from a day at the beach
my stamina is low, so I walk a little slower. I make it
a habit never to stand where I can be hit by tools.
Jesus gave us a very correct set of moral rules. Use them also.
Luke 2:47, *And all that heard him were*
astonished at his understanding and his answers.
I am writing quite a bit about alertness.

POSTCARDS FROM ZAKYNTHOS

for Ciaran Carson

Why would anyone post a postcard, when in the time it takes
the postmen of Europe to pass this photograph
of Solomos Square from hand to hand, from here to there,
my week's break in Zakynthos will be over?
Better to put it into your own hand, like this, in person,
with a duty-free gift of harsh cigarettes and ouzo.

What did I do on my holidays? I drank a beer called Mythos.
I swam and took the sun. I passed a glum taverna
called Nemesis and had this vision—table upon table
of the under-the-weather sipping local wine and wincing.
Oh how, they groan, are the mighty fallen, who whooped
it up, God's gifts, last night in Café Hubris.

Dionysios Solomos, national poet of Greece,
finished two poems only. After his death a disciple
gathered his odds and ends and made an *oeuvre*.
I think I will take this incompletist as a brother, sing
his praises in bursts and snapshots, bits and pieces.
Shore his fragments against my ruins.

The guidebook says Artemis, goddess of wildlife,
favoured Zakynthos. Janice breaks bread on our balcony
for finches and sparrows, feeds, against all advice,
the skinny cats, and swims while finches and sparrows
and skinny cats all sip together from the water
lapped over the edge of the pool with every stroke.

The statue of the poet in Solomos Square
is a statue of a sober gent, like Harland's statue
at the City Hall back home. A tobacco baron like his father?
That's the wisdom hinted at in Solomos, but
balanced by the firebrand, caution-to-the-wind forename.
How could he not be a dilettante, a dabbler?

Zante, *fior de Levante*, was earthquake-flattened
in 53. Pharmacist, scholar, Nikos Varvaris
rescued whatever was left of old Zakynthos—icons
and stonework shaken from churches, Italianate furniture, books.
For this he was christened the Knight of the Ruins.
There's someone else knew the value of salvage.

Below our studio door, the olive groves that,
as the guidebook says, abound with owls
are prowled this morning by an urgent cockerel and his dam.
Swallows take turns to skim the swimming pool,
each insect-kill an event horizon spreading through blue,
an aftershock shuddering across the tiles.

O biodiversity! The loggerhead turtle *Caretta caretta*
lays its eggs on beaches where us tourists
are forbidden to plant our parasols or build sandcastles.
One of their dwindling number, Paola, swims
with a radio beacon glued to her ancient shell.
A satellite picks up her bleeps: *I'm here … now here … now here.*

In the Museon Solomos the famous Zakynthians
have had their portraits painted by the same local artist:
unhandy, provincial, well aware of his limits.
Six notebook pages of the 'Hymn to Liberty' show
the poet skittering from Greek into Italian, back again,
dancing around the old fear of the demotic.

Shingle like lorry-loads of butter beans on Shipwreck
Cove, the water turquoise and bitterly cold.
The eponymous wreck's a rust-bucket smuggler—
unsalvaged monument to hubris. Better, it warns,
to work in a small way when the mood takes you,
than to go for one big score and run aground.

When the overweight man with the noisy children
belly-flops into the pool, the splash obscures
the name of the hotel tiled on the bottom. It means,
they tell me, 'welcome', but monoglot that I am
I translate it as 'stranger-love'. O etymology –
remind me again that we're all kin and all just tourists.

And so to the postcard: the tripod's set up on the northern
corner of Solomos Square, and a small crowd
of frock coats and curious hats squints at this oddball
recording nothing in particular for posterity.
How should they know that the earthquake is coming?
In fifty years, all this will be rubble.

Janice breaches the prohibition on kindness
to cats with a pinch of feta and tells me to send you her best.
The famous Zakynthians add their good wishes.
Dionysios Solomos reminds me that poetry's secret
is architecture, architecture and perseverance.
Many happy returns, he says. Wish you were here.

INTERNATIONAL THEOLOGICAL COMMISSION

THE HOPE OF SALVATION FOR INFANTS WHO DIE WITHOUT BEING BAPTISED

All booklets are published thanks to the generous support of the members of the Catholic Truth Society

CATHOLIC TRUTH SOCIETY
PUBLISHERS TO THE HOLY SEE